KS1 Maths (Year 1) Addition and Subtraction Workbook (Volume 1).

100 Maths practice worksheets (addition and subtraction, digits 0-10) and 25-word problems for reasoning, National curriculum, (Age 4-7)

Created by

Agnes Christy Books

(ACB)

100 pages of Addition and Subtraction worksheets and 25-word problems for reasoning.

(103 pages of homework (includes 100 pages of work sheets (2000 practice questions) and 3 pages of word problems for reasoning (25 questions). Answer key provided.)

This book will help the pupil to improve their speed and fluency in addition and subtraction skills (digits 0-10). The word problems will help them to develop reasoning and problem-solving skills. This book will provide additional practice for the students and compliment the schoolwork and help them to excel in maths.

The first 100 pages will help the children to become expert in basic addition and subtraction skills. At the end 25-word problems are given in the form of a story which will help the student to improve their reasoning and problem-solving skills and at the same time they can enjoy the story.

By practicing, revising, and repeating these questions will improve the children's addition and subtraction skills. This book can be used as a daily practice homework book (2 pages per day, will take 2 months to complete). Excellent practice workbook for year 1 students (KS1 National Curriculum, Age 4-7) to boost their confidence. There are no pictures or diagrams.

We believe that getting basics right will help them to have a bright future. After the completion of each page, use the reward page for colouring.

Content   Page

1)(Addition 0-2)

	A	B	C	D
1)	1+ 0=	2+0=	2+ 2=	2+1 =
2)	2+ 0=	1+1=	2+ 1=	1+ 2=
3)	2+ 1=	1+2=	2+ 1=	0+ 1=
4)	1+1 =	2+2=	2+1=	1+ 2=
5)	1+ 1=	2+ 2=	2+2=	2+ 0=
Date			Marks	/20

2)(Addition 0-2)

1)	**1+ 2=**	**2+ 2=**	**2+ 0=**	**2+0=**
2)	2+ 0=	2+2=	2+ 2=	0+0=
3)	2+2=	0+ 2=	1+ 2=	0+1=
4)	1+2=	1+0 =	0+1=	1+0=
5)	1+ 0=	0+ 0=	1+0=	2+2=
Date			Marks	/20

3(Addition 0-2)

1)	**1+ 0=**	**2+ 0=**	**1+ 0=**	**1+0=**
2)	2+ 0=	0+2=	0+ 2=	0+0=
3)	2+2=	0+ 2=	1+ 0=	0+0=
4)	1+0=	0+2 =	0+1=	1+0=
5)	0+ 0=	0+ 2=	1+0=	2+2=
Date			Marks	/20

4(Addition 0-2)

1)	1+ 2=	2+ 2=	1+ 0=	2+0=
2)	2+ 0=	2+2=	0+ 2=	0+0=
3)	2+2=	2+ 2=	2+ 2=	0+2=
4)	2+0=	2+2 =	0+1=	1+2=
5)	1+ 0=	2+ 2=	1+2=	2+2=
Date			Marks	/20

5(Addition 0-2)

1)	**1+ 1=**	**1+ 1=**	**1+ 0=**	**1+0=**
2)	1+ 0=	1+1=	0+ 1=	0+0=
3)	1+1=	0+ 1=	1+ 1=	0+1=
4)	1+0=	1+1 =	0+1=	1+1=
5)	1+ 0=	0+ 1=	1+1=	1+1=
Date			Marks	/20

6(Addition 0-2)

1)	**0+ 0=**	**2+ 1=**	**1+ 0=**	**1+0=**
2)	2+ 0=	1+0=	0+ 2=	0+0=
3)	2+2=	0+ 0=	1+ 1=	0+1=
4)	1+0=	0+0 =	0+1=	1+1=
5)	1+ 0=	0+ 2=	1+2=	0+0=
Date			Marks	/20

7) (Addition 0-2)

1)	**2+2=**	**0+ 1=**	**1+ 0=**	**1+0=**
2)	2+ 0=	2+2=	0+ 2=	0+0=
3)	2+2=	2+ 2=	1+ 1=	0+1=
4)	1+0=	2+2 =	0+0=	1+1=
5)	1+ 0=	0+ 2=	1+1=	2+2=
Date			Marks	/20

8) (Addition 0-2)

1)	**1+ 1=**	**2+ 1=**	**1+ 1=**	**1+0=**
2)	2+ 1=	1+1=	0+ 2=	0+0=
3)	2+2=	0+ 2=	1+ 1=	0+1=
4)	1+1=	1+2 =	0+1=	1+1=
5)	1+ 0=	0+ 2=	1+2=	0+0=
Date			Marks	/20

9) (Addition 0-2)

1)	**1+ 2=**	**2+ 2=**	**1+1=**	**0+0=**
2)	2+ 0=	1+0=	0+ 2=	0+0=
3)	2+2=	0+ 0=	1+0=	0+1=
4)	1+0=	1+0 =	0+1=	1+1=
5)	1+ 0=	0+ 0=	1+0=	1+2=
Date			Marks	/20

10) (Addition 0-2)

1)	**1+ 1=**	**1+ 1=**	**1+ 0=**	**1+0=**
2)	2+ 1=	1+1=	1+ 2=	0+0=
3)	2+2=	2+ 2=	1+ 1=	2+1=
4)	1+0=	1+1 =	0+2=	1+1=
5)	1+1=	1+ 2=	1+2=	2+2=
Date			Marks	/20

1)(Addition 0-5)

	A	B	C	D
1)	1+ 3=	2+4=	5+ 2=	5+ 5=
2)	2+ 0=	4+1=	5+ 1=	4+ 5=
3)	2+ 3=	4+2=	2+5=	3+ 4=
4)	1+3 =	2+2=	3+5=	4+ 5=
5)	1+ 3=	4+ 2=	5+4=	5+ 3=
Date			Marks	/20

2)(Addition 0-5)

	A	B	C	D
1)	1+ 5=	2+4=	5+ 3=	5+ 5=
2)	2+ 5=	4+1=	5+5=	4+ 5=
3)	2+ 3=	4+2=	2+5=	5+ 4=
4)	1+4 =	4+4=	3+5=	5+ 5=
5)	1+ 4=	4+ 2=	4+4=	5+ 3=
Date			Marks	/20

3)(Addition 0-5)

	A	B	C	D
1)	5+ 5=	2+4=	5+4=	5+ 5=
2)	2+ 4=	4+1=	5+ 3=	4+ 5=
3)	2+ 3=	4+2=	2+5=	3+ 4=
4)	3+4 =	2+2=	3+5=	4+ 5=
5)	3+ 5=	4+ 2=	5+4=	5+ 1=
Date			Marks	/20

4)(Addition 0-5)

	A	B	C	D
1)	5+ 3=	5+4=	5+2=	5+ 5=
2)	2+ 0=	4+4=	5+ 4=	4+ 5=
3)	2+ 3=	4+2=	2+5=	3+ 4=
4)	4+3 =	2+2=	4+5=	5+ 5=
5)	4+ 3=	4+ 2=	5+4=	5+ 1=
Date			Marks	/20

5)(Addition 0-5)

	A	B	C	D
1)	3+ 3=	5+4=	5+ 5=	5+ 5=
2)	5+ 0=	4+5=	5+ 5=	4+ 5=
3)	5+ 3=	4+5=	5+5=	3+ 4=
4)	1+5 =	5+2=	3+5=	4+ 5=
5)	1+ 3	4+5=	5+2=	4+ 3=
Date			Marks	/20

6)(Addition 0-5)

	A	B	C	D
1)	5+ 3=	5+4=	5+5=	0+ 5=
2)	2+ 0=	4+0=	5+ 1=	4+ 5=
3)	2+ 4=	4+5=	2+5=	3+ 4=
4)	1+3 =	0+2=	3+5=	4+ 5=
5)	1+ 3=	4+3=	5+0=	5+ 3=
Date			Marks	/20

7)(Addition 0-5)

	A	B	C	D
1)	1+ 0=	5+4=	5+ 3=	5+ 5=
2)	2+ 0=	4+1=	5+ 4=	5+ 5=
3)	2+ 3=	4+1=	1+5=	3+ 4=
4)	1+3 =	2+0=	3+5=	4+ 5=
5)	1+ 3=	4+ 3=	5+4=	0+ 3=
Date			Marks	/20

8)(Addition 0-5)

	A	B	C	D
1)	1+ 5=	2+4=	5+ 4=	5+ 5=
2)	2+ 0=	4+1=	5+ 1=	4+ 5=
3)	2+ 5=	4+2=	3+5=	3+ 4=
4)	1+3 =	2+4=	3+5=	4+ 5=
5)	1+ 5=	4+ 5=	5+4=	5+ 5=
Date			Marks	/20

9)(Addition 0-5)

	A	B	C	D
1)	1+ 3=	2+4=	5+ 2=	5+ 4=
2)	4+ 5=	4+1=	5+ 1=	4+ 5=
3)	5+ 3=	4+0=	0+5=	5+5=
4)	1+4 =	2+5=	3+5=	4+ 5=
5)	1+ 3=	4+ 2=	1+4=	5+ 4=
Date			Marks	/20

10)(Addition 0-5)

	A	B	C	D
1)	2+ 4=	2+3=	5+ 2=	5+ 1=
2)	4+ 0=	4+1=	4+ 2=	4+ 5=
3)	4+ 3=	4+4=	2+5=	3+ 5=
4)	1+5 =	5+2=	3+5=	4+ 5=
5)	1+ 3=	3+ 2=	3+4=	5+ 3=
Date			Marks	/20

11)(Addition 0-5)

	A	B	C	D
1)	1+ 3=	2+3=	5+ 3=	3+ 4=
2)	5+ 0=	5+1=	5+ 4=	5+ 5=
3)	4+ 3=	4+2=	4+5=	4+ 4=
4)	0+3 =	2+2=	3+3=	3+ 5=
5)	1+ 3=	4+ 3=	5+4=	5+ 5=
Date			Marks	/20

12)(Addition 0-5)

	A	B	C	D
1)	3+ 3=	2+4=	5+ 2=	5+ 5=
2)	2+ 0=	3+1=	5+ 4=	4+ 5=
3)	2+ 3=	5+2=	3+5=	3+ 4=
4)	1+5 =	2+2=	3+5=	3+ 5=
5)	1+ 3=	4+ 5=	5+4=	2+ 3=
Date			Marks	/20

13)(Addition 0-5)

	A	B	C	D	
1)	5+ 3=	2+4=	5+ 2=	5+ 3=	
2)	2+ 0=	4+5=	5+ 3=	4+ 5=	
3)	2+ 3=	4+3=	2+5=	3+ 4=	
4)	3+3 =	2+2=	3+5=	5+ 5=	
5)	3+ 3=	4+ 2=	5+4=	1+ 3=	
Date			Marks	/20	

14)(Addition 0-5)

	A	B	C	D
1)	4+ 4=	2+4=	5+ 2=	5+ 0=
2)	2+ 0=	4+4=	5+ 1=	4+ 5=
3)	2+ 3=	4+1=	4+5=	3+ 4=
4)	1+5 =	2+2=	3+5=	4+ 3=
5)	1+ 3=	4+ 0=	5+4=	5+ 0=
Date			Marks	/20

15)(Addition 0-5)

	A	B	C	D	
1)	1+ 1=	2+4=	5+ 2=	2+ 5=	
2)	2+ 2=	0+1=	5+ 2=	4+ 5=	
3)	0+ 3=	4+2=	1+5=	3+ 4=	
4)	2+3 =	2+2=	3+5=	4+ 0=	
5)	0+ 3=	4+ 2=	5+4=	5+ 0=	
Date			Marks	/20	

16)(Addition 0-5)

	A	B	C	D
1)	1+ 5=	2+4=	5+ 2=	5+ 5=
2)	5+ 0=	4+5=	5+ 4=	4+ 5=
3)	2+ 3=	4+5=	2+5=	3+ 4=
4)	1+5 =	2+2=	3+5=	4+ 5=
5)	1+ 3=	5+ 2=	5+4=	5+ 5=
Date			Marks	/20

17)(Addition 0-5)

	A	B	C	D
1)	1+ 0=	2+4=	5+ 2=	5+0=
2)	2+ 0=	4+1=	5+ 1=	4+ 5=
3)	2+ 3=	0+2=	2+5=	0+ 4=
4)	1+3 =	2+2=	3+0=	0+ 5=
5)	1+ 3=	4+ 0=	5+4=	0+0=
Date			Marks	/20

18)(Addition 0-5)

	A	B	C	D
1)	1+ 0=	2+4=	5+ 2=	5+ 5=
2)	2+ 0=	0+0=	1+ 1=	4+ 5=
3)	3+ 3=	4+2=	2+2=	3+ 4=
4)	3+3 =	2+2=	3+3=	5+ 5=
5)	3+ 3=	4+4=	5+4=	5+ 3=
Date			Marks	/20

19)(Addition 0-5)

	A	B	C	D
1)	2+2=	0+4=	5+0=	5+ 5=
2)	2+ 0=	4+0=	5+ 0=	4+ 5=
3)	2+ 0=	4+2=	2+0=	3+ 4=
4)	1+0=	2+2=	3+0=	4+ 5=
5)	1+ 3=	4+ 0=	0+4=	5+0=
Date			Marks	/20

20)(Addition 0-5)

	A	B	C	D
1)	1+ 5=	5+4=	5+ 3=	5+ 5=
2)	2+ 0=	4+1=	5+ 4=	4+ 5=
3)	3+ 3=	4+4=	2+5=	3+ 4=
4)	1+3 =	2+2=	4+5=	4+ 5=
5)	5+ 3=	4+3=	5+4=	4+ 3=
Date			Marks	/20

1)(Addition 0-10)

	A	B	C	D
1)	8+ 3=	2+9=	5+ 6=	5+ 8=
2)	2+9=	4+6=	5+7=	8+ 5=
3)	3+6=	6+2=	6+5=	6+ 4=
4)	7+3 =	7+2=	7+5=	4+ 7=
5)	7+ 8=	7+10=	8+4=	5+ 8=
Date			Marks	/20

2)(Addition 0-10)

	A	B	C	D
1)	1+ 9=	8+4=	5+7=	5+ 5=
2)	9+ 8=	4+1=	5+ 8=	4+ 5=
3)	2+9=	4+2=	2+9=	3+ 9=
4)	1+3 =	2+2=	3+8=	4+ 5=
5)	1+ 3=	4+ 2=	5+7=	9+ 9=
Date			Marks	/20

3)(Addition 0-10)

	A	B	C	D
1)	6+ 9=	8+6=	5+7=	5+ 6=
2)	9+ 8=	4+6=	5+ 8=	6+ 5=
3)	6+9=	4+6=	6+9=	7+ 9=
4)	6+3 =	2+6=	6+8=	6+ 5=
5)	1+ 6=	4+ 6=	6+7=	9+ 9=
Date			Marks	/20

4)(Addition 0-10)

	A	B	C	D
1)	7+ 9=	8+7=	7+7=	5+ 7=
2)	7+ 8=	4+7=	5+ 7=	4+ 7=
3)	2+7=	4+7=	7+9=	3+ 7=
4)	1+7 =	7+2=	7+8=	7+ 5=
5)	7+ 3=	7+ 2=	7+7=	7+ 9=
Date			Marks	/20

5)(Addition 0-10)

	A	B	C	D
1)	1+ 8=	8+7=	5+7=	5+ 5=
2)	8+ 8=	7+1=	5+ 8=	4+ 5=
3)	2+9=	7+2=	2+8=	3+ 8=
4)	1+3 =	2+2=	3+8=	7+ 5=
5)	1+ 3=	4+10=	5+7=	9+ 8=
Date			Marks	/20

6)(Addition 0-10)

	A	B	C	D
1)	6+ 9=	8+4=	5+7=	5+ 5=
2)	9+ 8=	4+6=	5+ 8=	4+ 5=
3)	6+9=	4+2=	6+9=	3+ 9=
4)	6+3 =	6+2=	3+8=	4+ 5=
5)	1+ 3=	4+ 6=	5+7=	9+ 6=
Date			Marks	/20

7)(Addition 0-10)

	A	B	C	D
1)	7+ 9=	8+4=	5+7=	5+ 5=
2)	9+ 7=	4+7=	5+ 8=	4+ 5=
3)	2+9=	4+7=	7+9=	3+ 9=
4)	1+3 =	7+7=	3+8=	4+ 5=
5)	1+ 9=	4+ 7=	5+7=	9+ 9=
Date			Marks	/20

40

8)(Addition 0-10)

	A	B	C	D
1)	9+ 9=	8+4=	9+7=	9+ 5=
2)	9+ 7=	9+1=	5+9=	9+ 5=
3)	8+9=	4+9=	2+9=	3+ 9=
4)	10+9 =	2+9=	10+8=	4+ 5=
5)	1+ 3=	4+ 2=	9+7=	9+ 8=
Date			Marks	/20

9)(Addition 0-10)

	A	B	C	D
1)	1+ 8=	8+4=	8+7=	5+ 5=
2)	9+ 8=	4+8=	5+ 8=	4+ 5=
3)	2+9=	8+2=	2+9=	8+ 9=
4)	8+7 =	2+2=	3+8=	4+ 5=
5)	8+ 3=	4+ 8=	5+7=	7+ 9=
Date			Marks	/20

10)(Addition 0-10)

	A	B	C	D
1)	7+ 9=	8+7=	7+7=	5+ 5=
2)	9+ 8=	4+7=	7+ 8=	4+ 5=
3)	2+9=	7+2=	2+9=	3+ 9=
4)	1+3 =	7+10=	3+8=	4+ 5=
5)	1+ 3=	4+ 2=	5+7=	7+ 0=
Date			Marks	/20

11)(Addition 0-10)

	A	B	C	D
1)	1+6=	8+6=	6+7=	6+ 5=
2)	9+ 8=	6+1=	5+ 8=	6+ 5=
3)	0+6=	6+2=	2+9=	6+ 9=
4)	6+3 =	6+2=	3+8=	4+ 5=
5)	6+10=	4+ 6=	6+7=	6+ 6=
Date			Marks	/20

12)(Addition 0-10)

	A	B	C	D
1)	5+ 9=	8+5=	5+7=	5+ 8=
2)	9+10=	4+1=	5+ 8=	4+ 5=
3)	5+9=	4+5=	2+9=	5+ 7=
4)	5+10=	2+5=	3+8=	4+ 5=
5)	5+ 3=	4+ 5=	5+7=	9+ 5=
Date			Marks	/20

13)(Addition 0-10)

	A	B	C	D
1)	1+ 9=	8+4=	5+7=	5+ 5=
2)	9+ 8=	4+1=	5+ 8=	4+ 5=
3)	2+9=	4+2=	10+9=	3+ 9=
4)	1+10=	2+2=	10+8=	4+ 5=
5)	1+ 3=	4+ 8=	5+7=	8+8=
Date			Marks	/20

14)(Addition 0-10)

	A	B	C	D
1)	8+7=	8+10=	5+7=	5+ 5=
2)	9+ 8=	4+9=	5+ 8=	4+ 5=
3)	2+9=	4+10=	2+9=	3+ 9=
4)	1+3 =	2+9=	3+8=	4+ 5=
5)	9+8=	4+ 9=	5+7=	7+ 9=
Date			Marks	/20

15)(Addition 0-10)

	A	B	C	D
1)	5+ 9=	8+4=	10+7=	5+ 5=
2)	9+ 8=	4+1=	5+ 8=	4+ 5=
3)	2+9=	4+7=	2+7=	3+ 9=
4)	8+3 =	2+8=	3+8=	4+ 5=
5)	7+ 3=	4+ 9=	5+10=	9+ 9=
Date			Marks	/20

48

1) (Subtraction 0-2)

	A	B	C	D
1)	1- 0=	2-0=	2- 2=	2-0 =
2)	2- 0=	1-1=	2- 1=	2- 2=
3)	2- 1=	2-2=	2- 1=	2- 1=
4)	1-1 =	2-2=	2-1=	2- 2=
5)	1- 1=	2- 0=	2-2=	2- 0=
Date			Marks	/20

2(Subtraction 0-2)

	A	B	C	D	
1)	1- 1=	2-1=	2- 0=	1-0 =	
2)	2- 0=	1-1=	2- 2=	2- 0=	
3)	2- 1=	2-2=	0- 0=	2- 1=	
4)	1-1 =	2-2=	2-1=	2- 0=	
5)	1- 1=	2- 0=	2-2=	2- 0=	
Date			Marks	/20	

3) (Subtraction 0-2)

	A	B	C	D
1)	1- 0=	2-1=	2- 2=	2-0 =
2)	0- 0=	2-1=	2- 1=	1-1=
3)	2- 1=	2-2=	2- 1=	2- 1=
4)	1-0 =	2-2=	0-0=	2- 2=
5)	2- 1=	2- 2=	2-1=	0- 0=
Date			Marks	/20

4) (Subtraction 0-2)

	A	B	C	D
1)	0- 0=	2-0=	2- 2=	2-0 =
2)	2- 0=	2-1=	2- 1=	2- 2=
3)	2- 1=	2-2=	2- 1=	2- 1=
4)	1-1 =	2-1=	2-1=	2- 2=
5)	1- 1=	1- 0=	2-2=	0- 0=
Date			Marks	/20

5) (Subtraction 0-2)

	A	B	C	D
1)	1- 1=	2-0=	2- 2=	2-2 =
2)	2- 0=	1-0=	2- 1=	2- 2=
3)	2- 1=	2-2=	2- 1=	2- 0=
4)	1-0 =	2-2=	2-1=	2- 2=
5)	1- 1=	2- 0=	2-2=	0- 0=
Date			Marks	/20

6) (Subtraction 0-2)

	A	B	C	D
1)	0- 0=	2-0=	2- 2=	2-1 =
2)	2- 1=	1-1=	2- 1=	2- 2=
3)	2- 1=	2-2=	2- 1=	2- 1=
4)	1-1 =	2-2=	2-1=	2- 2=
5)	1- 1=	2- 0=	2-0=	2- 1=
Date			Marks	/20

1) (Subtraction 0-5)

	A	B	C	D
1)	4- 0=	2-0=	3- 2=	2-0 =
2)	2- 0=	1-1=	5- 1=	2- 2=
3)	2- 1=	4-2=	2- 1=	2- 1=
4)	1-1 =	2-2=	2-1=	2- 2=
5)	1- 1=	5- 0=	2-2=	5- 0=
Date			Marks	/20

2) (Subtraction 0-5)

	A	B	C	D	
1)	5- 0=	4-0=	4- 2=	3-0 =	
2)	4- 0=	5-1=	2- 1=	3- 2=	
3)	2- 1=	2-2=	4- 1=	2- 1=	
4)	5-1 =	4-2=	4-1=	2- 2=	
5)	5- 1=	2- 0=	2-2=	2- 0=	
Date			Marks	/20	

3) (Subtraction 0-5)

	A	B	C	D
1)	4- 0=	2-0=	2- 2=	5-4 =
2)	2- 0=	4-1=	4- 1=	4- 2=
3)	2- 1=	2-2=	2- 1=	3- 1=
4)	1-1 =	2-2=	4-1=	3- 2=
5)	1- 1=	2- 0=	5-2=	3- 0=
Date			Marks	/20

4)(Subtraction 0-5)

	A	B	C	D
1)	4- 3=	5-4=	5- 2=	5- 5=
2)	2- 0=	4-1=	5- 1=	4- 1=
3)	2- 1=	4-2=	5-5=	5- 4=
4)	5-3 =	4-2=	5-5=	4-4=
5)	5- 3=	4- 2=	5-4=	5- 3=
Date			Marks	/20

5)(Subtraction 0-5)

	A	B	C	D
1)	3- 3=	4-4=	4- 2=	5- 5=
2)	2- 0=	4-1=	4- 1=	4- 1=
3)	2- 1=	4-2=	5-5=	5- 4=
4)	5-3 =	4-2=	5-3=	4-4=
5)	5- 0=	4- 2=	5-1=	5- 3=
Date			Marks	/20

6)(Subtraction 0-5)

	A	B	C	D
1)	4- 3=	5-4=	3- 2=	4-3=
2)	2- 0=	4-1=	5- 4=	4- 1=
3)	2- 1=	5-2=	5-3=	5- 4=
4)	3-3 =	4-2=	5-5=	4-4=
5)	4- 3=	5- 2=	5-4=	3- 3=
Date			Marks	/20

7)(Subtraction 0-5)

	A	B	C	D
1)	5- 3=	5-4=	5- 2=	5- 5=
2)	5- 0=	3-1=	3- 1=	4- 1=
3)	2- 1=	2-2=	5-5=	5- 4=
4)	4-3 =	3-2=	5-5=	5-4=
5)	3- 3=	5- 2=	5-4=	4-3=
Date			Marks	/20

8)(Subtraction 0-5)

	A	B	C	D
1)	4- 1=	4-0=	2- 2=	5-3=
2)	2- 0=	4-0=	5- 4=	4- 3=
3)	2- 1=	4-3=	5-3=	5- 4=
4)	5-3 =	4-2=	5-2=	4-4=
5)	3- 3=	4- 2=	5-2=	5-0=
Date			Marks	/20

62

9)(Subtraction 0-5)

	A	B	C	D
1)	3- 3=	4-1=	2- 2=	5- 5=
2)	2- 0=	3-1=	5- 1=	4- 1=
3)	2- 1=	3-2=	5-5=	5- 4=
4)	5-3 =	3-2=	4-4=	4-4=
5)	5-5=	4- 1=	5-4=	5- 1=
Date			Marks	/20

10)(Subtraction 0-5)

	A	B	C	D
1)	3-1=	4-3=	3- 2=	5- 5=
2)	4- 2=	3-1=	5- 3=	4-2=
3)	2- 1=	3-2=	5-0=	4- 4=
4)	3-3 =	4-1=	5-5=	4-1=
5)	5- 1=	4- 0=	5-2=	5- 4=
Date			Marks	/20

11)(Subtraction 0-5)

	A	B	C	D
1)	2- 1=	3-2=	5- 2=	5-3=
2)	5- 0=	4-3=	5- 4=	2- 1=
3)	5- 1=	4-2=	5-0=	5- 4=
4)	5-1 =	2-2=	5-2=	4-4=
5)	5- 5=	4- 2=	5-1=	5-5=
Date			Marks	/20

12)(Subtraction 0-5)

	A	B	C	D
1)	5- 3=	5-4=	5- 2=	5- 5=
2)	2- 1=	4-1=	5- 1=	4- 1=
3)	2- 1=	4-2=	3-1=	5- 4=
4)	3-3 =	4-2=	3-2=	4-4=
5)	3- 3=	4- 2=	3-3=	3-2=
Date			Marks	/20

13)(Subtraction 0-5)

	A	B	C	D
1)	5- 3=	5-4=	4- 2=	5- 5=
2)	2- 0=	4-1=	4- 2=	4- 1=
3)	2- 1=	4-2=	2-1=	5- 4=
4)	5-3 =	5-2=	5-0=	4-4=
5)	5- 1=	5- 2=	5-4=	5- 3=
Date			Marks	/20

14)(Subtraction 0-5)

	A	B	C	D
1)	1-1=	5-0=	3- 2=	2-2=
2)	2- 0=	4-3=	5- 5=	4- 3=
3)	2- 1=	4-0=	5-3=	5- 4=
4)	5-0 =	4-1=	2-2=	4-4=
5)	5- 3=	4- 0=	4-4=	5- 3=
Date			Marks	/20

15)(Subtraction 0-5)

	A	B	C	D
1)	3- 3=	3-0=	2-1=	5-3=
2)	2- 1=	4-4=	1- 1=	4-4 =
3)	2- 2=	4-3=	5-3=	5- 4=
4)	5-3 =	4-2=	3-3=	4-4=
5)	5- 5=	4-0=	5-4=	1-1=
Date			Marks	/20

16)(Subtraction 0-5)

	A	B	C	D
1)	4- 3=	5-4=	5- 2=	5- 5=
2)	2- 1=	4-1=	5- 1=	4- 1=
3)	2- 0=	4-2=	5-0=	5- 4=
4)	5-3 =	4-2=	3-3=	4-4=
5)	5- 3=	4- 2=	5-0=	5-4=
Date			Marks	/20

1)(Subtraction 0-10)

	A	B	C	D
1)	8- 3=	7-4=	5- 2=	5- 5=
2)	2- 0=	4-1=	6- 1=	4- 1=
3)	2- 1=	10-2=	6-5=	7- 4=
4)	6-3 =	4-2=	6-5=	4-4=
5)	5- 3=	4- 2=	5-4=	8- 3=
Date			Marks	/20

2)(Subtraction 0-10)

	A	B	C	D	
1)	8- 3=	8-4=	5- 2=	7- 5=	
2)	2- 0=	4-1=	8- 1=	4- 1=	
3)	2- 1=	4-2=	9-5=	5- 4=	
4)	7-3 =	7-2=	8-4=	8-4=	
5)	10-3=	9- 2=	5-4=	5- 3=	
Date			Marks	/20	

3)(Subtraction 0-10)

	A	B	C	D
1)	10-3=	9-4=	5- 2=	5- 5=
2)	2- 0=	9-1=	5- 1=	4- 1=
3)	2- 1=	4-2=	10-5=	5- 4=
4)	5-3 =	4-2=	8-5=	4-4=
5)	9- 3=	9- 2=	6-4=	7- 3=
Date			Marks	/20

4)(Subtraction 0-10)

	A	B	C	D
1)	9- 3=	8-4=	7- 2=	9- 5=
2)	2- 0=	4-1=	9- 1=	8- 1=
3)	2- 1=	9-2=	9-5=	5- 4=
4)	10-3=	9-5=	6-5=	8-4=
5)	8- 3=	4- 2=	6-4=	9- 3=
Date			Marks	/20

5)(Subtraction 0-10)

	A	B	C	D
1)	9- 3=	9-4=	9- 2=	10-5=
2)	8- 0=	9-1=	9- 1=	6- 1=
3)	7- 1=	4-2=	5-5=	9- 4=
4)	6-3 =	6-2=	5-5=	7-4=
5)	5- 3=	8- 2=	5-4=	7- 3=
Date			Marks	/20

6)(Subtraction 0-10)

	A	B	C	D
1)	10-3=	5-4=	5- 2=	9- 5=
2)	7- 0=	10-1=	9- 1=	8- 1=
3)	2- 1=	9-2=	10-5=	5- 4=
4)	9-3 =	4-2=	5-5=	10-4=
5)	5- 3=	8- 2=	5-4=	9- 3=
Date			Marks	/20

7)(Subtraction 0-10)

	A	B	C	D
1)	9- 9=	8-4=	5-3=	6- 5=
2)	9- 8=	4-1=	10- 8=	9- 5=
3)	10-9=	9-2=	8-7=	7-6=
4)	9-3 =	8-2=	7-4=	8- 5=
5)	10-3=	4- 2=	7-7=	9- 9=
Date			Marks	/20

8)(Subtraction 0-10)

	A	B	C	D
1)	9- 7=	8-4=	9-3=	8- 5=
2)	9- 8=	7-1=	10- 8=	9- 5=
3)	10-9=	9-2=	7-7=	7-6=
4)	9-3 =	8-2=	7-4=	8- 5=
5)	10-3=	4- 2=	7-7=	9- 7=
Date			Marks	/20

9)(Subtraction 0-10)

	A	B	C	D
1)	9- 2=	8-4=	5-3=	5- 5=
2)	9- 8=	8-1=	10- 8=	9- 5=
3)	10-9=	9-2=	8-7=	7-6=
4)	7-3 =	6-2=	9-4=	8- 5=
5)	10-3=	4- 2=	7-7=	9- 3=
Date			Marks	/20

10)(Subtraction 0-10)

	A	B	C	D
1)	9- 5=	8-4=	8-3=	6- 5=
2)	9- 8=	4-1=	10- 8=	9- 5=
3)	10-9=	9-6=	8-3=	7-6=
4)	9-7 =	8-2=	7-6=	8- 5=
5)	7-3=	4- 2=	7-1=	9- 3=
Date			Marks	/20

11)(Subtraction 0-10)

	A	B	C	D
1)	9- 3=	8-3=	5-3=	6- 5=
2)	9- 8=	4-1=	10-6=	9- 5=
3)	10-6=	9-2=	8-4=	7-6=
4)	9-3 =	8-2=	9-4=	8- 5=
5)	9-3=	4- 2=	7-5=	9-4=
Date			Marks	/20

12)(Subtraction 0-10)

	A	B	C	D
1)	6- 2=	8-4=	5-3=	6- 5=
2)	9- 8=	10-8=	10-6=	9- 5=
3)	6-4=	9-2=	8-7=	7-6=
4)	8-3 =	8-2=	7-7=	8- 5=
5)	10-3=	4- 2=	7-3=	8- 4=
Date			Marks	/20

13)(Subtraction 0-10)

	A	B	C	D
1)	7-4 =	8-4=	5-3=	9- 5=
2)	8-5=	4-1=	10- 8=	9- 5=
3)	9-2=	9-5=	8-4=	7-6=
4)	8-3 =	8-2=	7-3=	8- 5=
5)	7-3=	4- 2=	7-4=	7- 2=
Date			Marks	/20

14)(Subtraction 0-10)

	A	B	C	D
1)	8-5=	8-1=	5-3=	5- 5=
2)	9- 8=	4-1=	10- 8=	9- 5=
3)	10-9=	8-2=	8-7=	7-6=
4)	9-3 =	8-2=	10-4=	8- 5=
5)	10-3=	4- 2=	10-7=	10-9=
Date			Marks	/20

15)(Subtraction 0-10)

	A	B	C	D
1)	6-6=	6-4=	6-3=	6- 5=
2)	8- 8=	8-1=	10- 8=	8- 5=
3)	10-9=	7-2=	7-7=	7-6=
4)	9-3 =	9-2=	9-4=	9- 5=
5)	10-3=	4- 2=	7-7=	7-1=
Date			Marks	/20

1)(Mixed operations 0-10)

	A	B	C	D
1)	9+ 9=	8-4=	5-3=	6- 2=
2)	9+ 8=	4-1=	10- 8=	9- 5=
3)	10-9=	9-2=	8+7=	7-6=
4)	9-3 =	8-2=	7-4=	8- 5=
5)	10-8=	4- 2=	7+7=	9-6=
Date			Marks	/20

2)(Mixed operations 0-10)

	A	B	C	D
1)	9- 2=	8-4=	5-3=	6+ 5=
2)	9- 8=	4+1=	10- 8=	9- 5=
3)	10-9=	9+2=	8-7=	7-6=
4)	9-3 =	8-2=	7-4=	8+ 5=
5)	10-2=	4+ 2=	7-7=	9 +9=
Date			Marks	/20

3)(Mixed operations 0-10)

	A	B	C	D
1)	10-2=	8-4=	5-3=	10+5=
2)	9- 8=	9-3=	10+ 8=	9- 5=
3)	10-9=	9+2=	8-4=	7-6=
4)	9-3 =	8+2=	7-4=	7- 5=
5)	10-3=	4+9=	7-7=	9-5=
Date			Marks	/20

4)Mixed operations (0-10)

	A	B	C	D
1)	9+ 5=	8-5=	5+3=	7- 5=
2)	9+8=	4-2=	10+ 8=	10-5=
3)	10+9=	9-3=	8+7=	8-6=
4)	9+3 =	8-3=	7+4=	9- 5=
5)	10+3=	4- 3=	7+7=	10-9=
Date			Marks	/20

5)(Mixed operations 0-10)

	A	B	C	D
1)	8+8=	8+4=	5-3=	6- 5=
2)	9- 8=	4-1=	10+ 8=	9- 5=
3)	10-9=	9-2=	8+7=	7-6=
4)	8-3 =	8-2=	7+5=	8- 5=
5)	10-4=	4+6=	7+8=	9- 9=
Date			Marks	/20

6)(Mixed operations 0-10)

	A	B	C	D
1)	7-2=	9-4=	6+3=	6-1=
2)	9- 8=	9+9=	10- 8=	9+5=
3)	10+10=	9-2=	8-7=	7-6=
4)	9-3 =	8-2=	7-4=	8- 5=
5)	10-3=	4+10=	7-7=	1-1=
Date			Marks	/20

7)(Mixed operations 0-10)

	A	B	C	D
1)	10-5=	8-4=	5-3=	6- 5=
2)	10- 8=	10+10=	10-1=	9- 5=
3)	10-10=	9-2=	10-0=	7+6=
4)	9-3 =	8-2=	10-4=	8- 5=
5)	10-0=	9- 7=	10-7=	10+ 9=
Date			Marks	/20

8)(Mixed operations 0-10)

	A	B	C	D
1)	6+ 9=	8-6=	5+6=	6- 5=
2)	9- 8=	4+6=	10- 7=	9-3=
3)	10+9=	9-2=	8-3=	7+6=
4)	9-2 =	8+2=	7-1=	8- 5=
5)	10-3=	4- 2=	7-7=	6+ 10=
Date			Marks	/20

9)(Mixed operations 0-10)

	A	B	C	D	
1)	9+ 9=	8-4=	5-3=	6-3=	
2)	9- 8=	4-1=	10- 8=	9- 5=	
3)	10-9=	9-2=	8+8=	7-6=	
4)	9-3 =	8-2=	7-0=	8- 5=	
5)	10-3=	4- 2=	7+9=	10-10=	
Date			Marks	/20	

10)(Mixed operations 0-10)

	A	B	C	D
1)	10-3=	7+9=	5+5=	6-0=
2)	8+ 8=	4+10=	10- 8=	9- 1=
3)	10+9=	9-2=	8+7=	7-6=
4)	9-4 =	8-3=	7+4=	8- 5=
5)	10-7=	8- 2=	3+7=	5+5=
Date			Marks	/20

11)(Mixed operations 0-10)

	A	B	C	D
1)	10-6=	9-4=	5-1=	6- 5=
2)	7- 4=	9+9=	10- 7=	9- 5=
3)	10-9=	9-4=	8-7=	7-6=
4)	9-2 =	8-1=	7-4=	8- 5=
5)	10-3=	4+ 2=	7-2=	9-2=
Date			Marks	/20

12)(Mixed operations 0-10)

	A	B	C	D
1)	1+ 9=	8+4=	5+7=	5+ 5=
2)	9-5=	4+1=	5+ 8=	4+ 5=
3)	2+9=	4+2=	2+9=	9- 9=
4)	1+3 =	2+2=	3+8=	4+ 5=
5)	1+ 3=	4+ 2=	5+7=	9-7=
Date			Marks	/20

13)(Mixed operations 0-10)

	A	B	C	D
1)	6+ 9=	8+4=	5+7=	5+ 5=
2)	9+ 8=	4+1=	5+ 8=	4+ 5=
3)	2+9=	10-2=	2+9=	3+ 9=
4)	1+3 =	8-2=	3+8=	4+ 5=
5)	1+ 3=	4+ 2=	5+7=	10-1=
Date			Marks	/20

14)(Mixed operations 0-10)

	A	B	C	D
1)	8+ 9=	7+4=	5+7=	5+ 5=
2)	10-8=	4+1=	5+ 8=	4+ 5=
3)	9+9=	4+2=	2+9=	3+ 9=
4)	1+3 =	6-2=	10+8=	4+ 5=
5)	10+0=	4+ 2=	9-7=	9-2=
Date			Marks	/20

15) (Mixed operations 0-10)

	A	B	C	D
1)	1+ 9=	8+4=	5+7=	5+ 5=
2)	9+ 8=	4+1=	5+ 8=	4+ 5=
3)	2+9=	4+2=	2+9=	3+ 9=
4)	1+3 =	2+2=	3+8=	4+ 5=
5)	1+ 3=	4+ 2=	5+7=	9+ 9=
Date			Marks	/20

16)(Mixed operations 0-10)

	A	B	C	D
1)	6+ 1=	8+4=	5+7=	5+ 9=
2)	9+ 8=	4+1=	1+ 8=	4+ 5=
3)	2+9=	10-2=	2+6=	3+ 9=
4)	1+3 =	8-2=	3+8=	4+ 5=
5)	1+ 9=	4+8=	5+9=	10-1=
Date			Marks	/20

17)(Mixed operations 0-10)

	A	B	C	D
1)	10-1=	6+9=	5+8=	6-0=
2)	8+ 9=	3+10=	10- 8=	9- 2=
3)	10+6=	9-3=	8+7=	7-6=
4)	9-4 =	8-2=	9+4=	8- 5=
5)	10-5=	8- 0=	3+7=	5+0=
Date			Marks	/20

18)(Mixed operations 0-10)

	A	B	C	D
1)	10-2=	7+9=	5+5=	6-3=
2)	7+7=	4+9=	10- 1=	8- 2=
3)	10+1=	9-0=	10+7=	9-6=
4)	8-4 =	6-2=	7+4=	9- 5=
5)	9-1=	7- 7=	4+8=	5+5=
Date			Marks	/20

The Magic Cave

Word problems (0-5 Addition challenge)

1)Anna and Ben wanted to climb the tall mountain. They know that there is a magic cave on the top of the mountain and there lived a magic wise cat. They were eager to see the wise cat, so they set out for the journey. Ben packed 2 bags and Anna packed 2 bags. How many bags did they pack altogether?

2)Anna has 1 water bottle in her bag and Ben has 2 water bottles in his bag. How many water bottles did they have altogether?

3)Anna has 5 oranges in her bag and Ben has 4 oranges in his bag. How many oranges did they have altogether?

4) Anna has 4 buns in her bag and Ben has 4 buns in his bag. How many buns did they have altogether?

5)On the way to the mountain they saw 5 blue butterflies and 3 yellow butterflies. How many butterflies did they see altogether?

6)On the way to mountain they stopped by a river. They saw lots of beautiful flowers at the bank of the river. Anna picked 4 red flowers and Ben picked 3 yellow flowers. How many flowers did they pick altogether?

Word problems (0-10 Addition challenge)

7)By the river Ben and Anna collected stones and they wanted to throw it in the river. Ben collected 7 stones. Anna collected 9 stones. How many did they collect altogether?

8)They saw many fish in the river. Ann counted 9 blue fish and Ben counted 6 orange fish. How many fish did they count altogether?

9) Ann caught 5 fish and Ben caught 9 fish. Together how many fish did they catch?

10) Ben has 9 fish, he put 7 fish back in to the river, so how many fish did he have now?

Word problems (Subtraction 0-10 challenge)

11)Ben has two fish with him. He put two fish back in the river. How many fish did he have now?

12)Ann and Ben continued their journey and they found an apple tree. They picked 4 apples from the tree. Ben ate 1 apple and Anna ate one apple. How many apples left with them now?

13)Ben has 5 sweets in his pocket. He gave 3 of them to Ann. How many sweets left in his pocket now?

14)Ann has 4 chocolates in her bag. She gave one chocolate to Ben. How many chocolates left in her bag?

15)Ann and Ben have 9 oranges in their bag. They ate 5 oranges. How many oranges are left in their bag?

16)Ben and Ann sat under a tree. They looked up and saw 9 beautiful birds sitting on the tree. After some time 3 of them flew away. How many birds are still sitting on the tree?

17) They saw two birds' nest on the tree, and they found grey and white eggs inside the nests. There were 10 eggs. 7 of them were grey. How many white eggs did they find inside the nest?

18)Ben tried to climb on the tree. Then a small branch with yellow and green leaves fallout from the tree. Anna counted the leaves on the branch. There were 10 leaves and 5 of them were green. How many yellow leaves did Anna find on the branch?

19)Ben got down from the tree. He saw the small branch with 10 leaves. He liked the yellow leaves, so he picked one yellow leaf from the branch. How many leaves left on the branch?

20) Ben and Ann saw lot of ants under the tree. Some of them were red and others were black. They looked at the ants. Ann found 9 black ants. 3 of the black ants were little and the remaining were big. How many big black ants did Ann find under the tree?

21) Ben found 10 red ants. 2 of them were little and the remaining were big. How many big red ants did Ben find under the tree?

22) Ben and Ann continued their journey. They found 10 white steps to reach the mountain. They climbed 3 steps. How many more steps do they need to climb to reach the top of the mountain.

23) At last they reached in front of the cave. They found 5 golden bells and 10 silver bells in front of the cave. In total, how many bells did they find in front of the cave?

24) Ann rang the bell. Suddenly the door opened by itself. Then they saw 9 chairs. Some of them were black and remaining were white. They noticed that 7 of them were white. How many black chairs did they find?

25) Suddenly Ben and Ann heard a voice. 'I am the wise cat welcome to my magic cave, sit down and wait, I will be coming soon'. Ann and Benn waited eagerly to see the wise cat. Slowly the wise cat appeared in front of them, he was so beautiful, and he was wearing a magic bell on his neck. I could give you anything you want; I am the magic wise cat. What can I do for you today? Asked the wise cat.

Ben looked at Ann and said, how can we become the best in mathematics. We both want to be the best in mathematics. The wise cat laughed loudly and said, **PRACTICE, PRACTICE, PRACTICE**. The more you practice the better. If you practice maths will become so easy for you and you will love it so much. Hearing this Ann and Ben become so happy and decided to practice maths every single day. The wise cat gave them 10 pieces of cake. Ben had 6 of the cakes and Ann had the rest. How many cakes did Ann eat?

Answers (Page no 4-23)

Page no-4	A	B	C	D	Page no-5	A	B	C	D	Page no-6	A	B	C	D	Page no-7	A	B	C	D
1)	1	2	4	3	1)	3	4	2	2	1)	1	2	1	1	1)	3	4	1	2
2)	2	2	3	3	2)	2	4	4	0	2)	2	2	2	0	2)	2	4	2	0
3)	3	3	3	1	3)	4	2	3	1	3)	4	2	1	0	3)	4	4	4	2
4)	2	4	3	3	4)	3	1	1	1	4)	1	2	1	1	4)	2	4	1	3
5)	2	4	4	2	5)	1	0	1	4	5)	0	2	1	4	5)	1	4	3	4

Page no-8	A	B	C	D	Page no-9	A	B	C	D	Page no-10	A	B	C	D	Page no-11	A	B	C	D
1)	2	2	1	1	1)	0	3	1	1	1)	4	1	1	1	1)	2	3	2	1
2)	1	2	1	0	2)	2	1	2	0	2)	2	4	2	0	2)	3	2	2	0
3)	2	1	2	1	3)	4	0	2	1	3)	4	4	2	1	3)	4	2	2	1
4)	1	2	1	2	4)	1	0	1	2	4)	1	4	0	2	4)	2	3	1	2
5)	1	1	2	2	5)	1	2	3	0	5)	1	2	2	4	5)	1	2	3	0

Page -12	A	B	C	D	Page 13	A	B	C	D	Page 14	A	B	C	D	Page 15	A	B	C	D
1)	3	4	2	0	1)	2	2	1	1	1)	4	6	7	10	1)	6	6	8	10
2)	2	1	2	0	2)	3	2	3	0	2)	2	5	6	9	2)	7	5	10	9
3)	4	0	1	1	3)	4	4	2	3	3)	3	6	7	7	3)	5	6	7	9
4)	1	1	1	2	4)	1	2	2	1	4)	4	4	5	9	4)	5	8	8	10
5)	1	0	1	3	5)	2	3	3	4	5)	4	6	9	8	5)	5	6	8	8

Page 16	A	B	C	D	Page 17	A	B	C	D	Page 18	A	B	C	D	Page 19	A	B	C	D
1)	10	6	9	10	1)	8	9	10	10	1)	6	9	10	10	1)	8	9	10	5
2)	6	5	8	9	2)	2	8	9	9	2)	5	9	10	9	2)	2	4	6	9
3)	3	6	7	7	3)	5	6	7	7	3)	8	9	10	7	3)	6	9	7	7
4)	7	4	8	9	4)	7	4	9	10	4)	6	7	8	9	4)	4	2	8	9
5)	8	6	9	6	5)	7	6	9	6	5)	4	9	7	7	5)	4	7	5	8

Page 20	A	B	C	D	Page 21	A	B	C	D	Page 22	A	B	C	D	Page 23	A	B	C	D
1)	1	9	8	10	1)	6	6	9	10	1)	4	6	7	9	1)	6	5	7	6
2)	2	5	9	10	2)	2	5	6	9	2)	9	5	6	9	2)	4	5	6	9
3)	5	5	6	7	3)	7	6	8	7	3)	8	4	5	1	3)	7	8	7	8
4)	4	2	8	9	4)	4	6	8	9	4)	5	7	8	9	4)	6	7	8	9
5)	4	7	9	3	5)	6	9	9	10	5)	4	6	5	9	5)	4	5	7	8

Answers (Page no 24-33)

Page no-24					Page no-25					Page no-26					Page no-27			
	A	B	C	D		A	B	C	D		A	B	C	D		A	B	C	D
1)	1	2	4	3	1)	6	6	7	10	1)	8	6	7	8	1)	8	6	7	5
2)	2	2	3	3	2)	2	4	9	9	2)	2	9	8	9	2)	2	8	6	9
3)	3	3	3	1	3)	5	7	8	7	3)	5	7	7	7	3)	5	5	9	7
4)	2	4	3	3	4)	6	4	8	8	4)	6	4	8	10	4)	6	4	8	7
5)	2	4	4	2	5)	4	9	9	5	5)	6	6	9	4	5)	4	4	9	5
Page no-28	A	B	C	D	Page no-29	A	B	C	D	Page no-30	A	B	C	D	Page no-31	A	B	C	D
1)	2	6	7	7	1)	6	6	7	10	1)	1	6	7	5	1)	1	6	7	10
2)	4	1	7	9	2)	5	9	9	9	2)	2	5	6	9	2)	2	0	2	9
3)	3	6	6	7	3)	5	9	7	7	3)	5	2	7	4	3)	6	6	4	7
4)	5	4	8	4	4)	6	4	8	9	4	4	4	3	5	4)	6	4	6	10
5)	3	6	9	5	5)	4	7	9	10	5)	4	4	9	0	5)	6	8	9	8
Page 32	A	B	C	D	Page 33	A	B	C	D										
1)	4	4	5	10	1)	6	9	8	10										
2)	2	4	5	9	2)	2	5	9	9										
3)	2	6	2	7	3)	6	8	7	7										
4)	1	4	3	9	4)	4	4	9	9										
5)	4	4	4	5	5)	8	7	9	7										

Answers (Page no 34-48)

Page no-34	A	B	C	D	Page no-35	A	B	C	D	Page no-36	A	B	C	D
1)	11	11	11	13	1)	10	12	12	10	1)	15	14	12	11
2)	11	10	12	13	2)	17	5	13	9	2)	17	10	13	11
3)	9	8	11	10	3)	11	6	11	12	3)	15	10	15	16
4)	10	9	12	11	4)	4	4	12	9	4)	9	8	14	11
5)	15	17	12	13	5)	4	6	12	18	5)	7	10	13	18
Page no-37	A	B	C	D	Page no-38	A	B	C	D	Page no-39	A	B	C	D
1)	16	15	14	12	1)	9	15	12	10	1)	15	12	12	10
2)	15	11	12	11	2)	16	8	13	9	2)	17	10	13	9
3)	9	11	16	10	3)	11	9	10	11	3)	15	6	15	12
4)	8	9	15	12	4)	4	4	11	12	4)	9	8	11	9
5)	10	8	14	16	5)	4	14	12	17	5)	4	10	12	15
Page 40	A	B	C	D	Page 41	A	B	C	D	Page 42	A	B	C	D
1)	16	12	12	10	1)	18	12	16	14	1)	9	12	15	10
2)	16	11	13	9	2)	16	10	14	14	2)	17	12	13	9
3)	11	11	16	12	3)	17	13	11	12	3)	11	10	11	17
4)	4	14	11	9	4)	19	11	18	9	4)	15	4	11	9
5)	10	11	12	18	5)	4	6	16	17	5)	11	12	12	16
Page 43	A	B	C	D	Page 44	A	B	C	D	Page 45	A	B	C	D
1)	11	15	14	10	1)	7	14	13	11	1)	14	13	12	13
2)	17	11	15	9	2)	17	07	13	11	2)	19	5	13	9
3)	11	9	11	12	3)	6	8	11	15	3)	14	9	11	12
4)	4	17	11	9	4)	9	8	11	9	4)	15	7	11	9
5)	4	6	12	7	5)	16	10	13	12	5)	8	9	12	14
Page 46	A	B	C	D	Page 47	A	B	C	D	Page 48	A	B	C	D
1)	10	12	12	10	1)	15	18	12	10	1)	14	12	17	10
2)	17	5	13	9	2)	17	13	13	9	2)	17	5	13	9
3)	11	6	19	12	3)	11	14	11	12	3)	11	11	9	12
4)	11	4	18	9	4)	4	11	11	9	4)	11	10	11	9
5)	4	12	12	16	5)	17	13	12	16	5)	10	13	15	18

Answers (Page no 49-68)

Page no-49					Page no-50					Page no-51					Page no-52				
	A	B	C	D		A	B	C	D		A	B	C	D		A	B	C	D
1)	1	2	0	2	1)	0	1	2	1	1)	1	1	0	2	1)	0	2	0	2
2)	2	0	1	0	2)	2	0	0	2	2)	0	1	1	0	2)	2	1	1	0
3)	1	0	1	1	3)	1	0	0	1	3)	1	0	1	1	3)	1	0	1	1
4)	0	0	1	0	4)	0	0	1	2	4)	1	0	0	0	4)	0	1	1	0
5)	0	2	0	2	5)	0	2	0	2	5)	1	0	1	0	5)	0	1	0	0
Page no-53	A	B	C	D	Page no-54	A	B	C	D	Page no-55	A	B	C	D	Page no-56	A	B	C	D
1)	0	2	0	0	1)	0	2	0	1	1)	4	2	1	2	1)	5	4	2	3
2)	2	1	1	0	2)	1	0	1	0	2)	2	0	4	0	2)	4	4	1	1
3)	1	0	1	2	3)	1	0	1	1	3)	1	2	1	1	3)	1	0	3	1
4)	1	0	1	0	4)	0	0	1	0	4	0	0	1	0	4)	4	2	3	0
5)	0	2	0	0	5)	0	2	2	1	5)	0	5	0	5	5)	4	2	0	2
Page 57	A	B	C	D	Page 58	A	B	C	D	Page 59	A	B	C	D	Page 60	A	B	C	D
1)	4	2	0	1	1)	1	1	3	0	1)	0	0	2	0	1)	1	1	1	1
2)	2	3	3	2	2)	2	3	4	3	2)	2	3	3	3	2)	2	3	1	3
3)	1	0	1	2	3)	1	2	0	1	3)	1	2	0	1	3)	1	3	2	1
4)	0	0	3	1	4)	1	2	0	0	4)	2	2	1	0	4)	0	2	0	0
5)	0	2	3	3	5)	1	2	1	2	5)	5	2	4	2	5)	1	3	1	0
Page 61	A	B	C	D	Page 62	A	B	C	D	Page 63	A	B	C	D	Page 64	A	B	C	D
1)	2	1	3	0	1)	3	4	0	2	1)	0	3	0	0	1)	2	1	1	0
2)	5	2	2	3	2)	2	4	1	1	2)	2	2	4	3	2)	2	2	2	2
3)	1	0	0	1	3)	1	1	1	1	3)	1	1	0	1	3)	1	1	5	0
4)	1	1	0	1	4)	2	2	3	0	4)	2	1	0	0	4)	0	3	0	3
5)	6	3	1	1	5)	0	2	3	5	5)	0	3	1	4	5)	4	4	3	1
Page 65	A	B	C	D	Page 66	A	B	C	D	Page 67	A	B	C	D	Page 68	A	B	C	D
1)	1	1	3	2	1)	2	1	3	0	1)	2	1	2	0	1)	0	5	1	0
2)	5	1	1	1	2)	1	3	4	3	2)	2	3	2	3	2)	2	1	0	1
3)	4	2	5	1	3)	1	2	2	1	3)	1	2	1	1	3)	1	4	2	1
4)	4	0	3	0	4)	0	2	1	0	4)	1	3	5	0	4)	5	3	0	0
5)	0	2	4	0	5)	0	2	0	1	5)	4	3	1	2	5)	2	4	0	2

Answers (Page no 69-86)

Page no-69	A	B	C	D	Page no-70	A	B	C	D	Page no-71	A	B	C	D	Page no-72	A	B	C	D
1)	0	3	1	2	1)	1	1	3	0	1)	5	3	3	0	1)	5	4	3	2
2)	1	0	0	0	2)	1	3	4	3	2)	2	3	5	3	2)	2	3	9	3
3)	0	1	2	1	3)	2	2	5	1	3)	1	8	1	3	3)	1	2	4	1
4)	2	2	0	0	4)	2	2	0	0	4)	3	2	1	0	4)	4	5	4	4
5)	0	4	1	0	5)	2	2	5	1	5)	2	2	1	5	5)	7	7	1	2
Page no-73	A	B	C	D	Page no-74	A	B	C	D	Page no-75	A	B	C	D	Page no-76	A	B	C	D
1)	7	5	3	0	1)	6	4	5	4	1)	6	5	7	5	1)	7	1	3	4
2)	2	8	4	3	2)	2	3	8	7	2)	8	8	8	5	2)	7	9	8	7
3)	1	2	5	1	3)	1	7	4	1	3)	6	2	0	5	3)	1	7	5	1
4)	2	2	3	0	4)	7	4	1	4	4	3	4	0	3	4)	6	2	0	6
5)	6	7	2	4	5)	5	2	2	6	5)	2	6	1	4	5)	2	6	1	6
Page -77	A	B	C	D	Page 78	A	B	C	D	Page 79	A	B	C	D	Page 80	A	B	C	D
1)	0	4	2	1	1)	2	4	6	3	1)	7	4	2	0	1)	4	4	5	1
2)	1	3	2	1	2)	1	6	2	4	2)	1	7	2	4	2)	1	3	2	4
3)	1	7	2	1	3)	1	7	0	1	3)	1	7	1	1	3)	1	3	5	1
4)	6	6	3	3	4)	6	6	3	3	4)	4	4	5	3	4)	2	6	1	3
5)	7	2	0	0	5)	7	2	0	2	5)	7	2	0	6	5)	4	2	6	6
Page 81	A	B	C	D	Page 82	A	B	C	D	Page 83	A	B	C	D	Page 84	A	B	C	D
1)	6	5	2	1	1)	4	4	2	1	1)	3	4	2	4	1)	3	7	2	0
2)	1	3	4	4	2)	1	2	4	4	2)	3	3	2	4	2)	1	3	2	4
3)	4	7	4	1	3)	2	7	1	1	3)	7	4	4	1	3)	1	6	1	1
4)	6	6	5	3	4)	5	6	0	3	4)	5	6	4	3	4)	6	6	6	3
5)	6	2	2	5	5)	7	2	4	4	5)	4	2	3	5	5)	7	2	3	1
Page 85	A	B	C	D	Page 86	A	B	C	D										
1)	0	2	3	1	1)	18	4	2	4										
2)	0	7	2	3	2)	17	3	2	4										
3)	1	5	0	1	3)	1	7	15	1										
4)	6	7	5	4	4)	6	6	3	3										
5)	7	2	0	6	5)	2	2	14	3										

Answers (Page no 87-103)

Page.87	A	B	C	D		Page.88	A	B	C	D		Page.89	A	B	C	D
1)	7	4	2	11		1)	8	4	2	15		1)	14	3	8	2
2)	1	5	2	4		2)	1	6	18	4		2)	17	2	18	5
3)	1	1	1	1		3)	1	11	4	1		3)	19	6	15	2
4)	6	6	3	13		4)	6	10	3	2		4)	12	5	11	4
5)	8	6	0	18		5)	7	13	0	4		5)	13	1	14	1
Page 90	A	B	C	D		Page 91	A	B	C	D		Page 92	A	B	C	D
1)	16	12	2	1		1)	5	5	9	5		1)	5	4	2	1
2)	1	3	18	1		2)	1	18	2	14		2)	2	20	9	4
3)	1	7	15	1		3)	20	7	1	1		3)	0	7	10	13
4)	5	6	12	3		4)	6	6	3	3		4	4	6	6	3
5)	6	10	15	0		5)	7	14	0	0		5)	10	2	3	19

Page 93	A	B	C	D		Page 94	A	B	C	D		Page 94	A	B	C	D
1)	15	2	11	1		1)	18	4	2	3		1)	18	4	2	3
2)	1	10	3	6		2)	1	3	2	4		2)	1	3	2	4
3)	19	7	5	13		3)	1	1	16	1		3)	1	1	16	1
4)	7	10	6	3		4)	6	6	7	3		4)	6	6	7	3
5)	7	2	0	16		5)	7	2	16	0		5)	7	2	16	0
Page 95	A	B	C	D		Page 96	A	B	C	D		Page 97	A	B	C	D
1)	7	16	10	6		1)	4	5	4	1		1)	10	12	12	10
2)	16	14	2	8		2)	3	18	3	4		2)	2	5	13	9
3)	19	7	15	1		3)	1	5	1	1		3)	11	6	11	0
4)	5	5	11	3		4)	7	7	3	3		4)	4	4	11	9
5)	3	6	10	10		5)	7	6	5	7		5)	4	6	12	2
Page 98	A	B	C	D		Page 99	A	B	C	D		Page 100	A	B	C	D
1)	15	12	12	10		1)	17	11	12	10		1)	9	5	15	15
2)	17	5	13	9		2)	2	5	13	9		2)	3	5	13	5
3)	11	8	11	12		3)	18	6	11	12		3)	6	6	11	6
4)	4	6	11	9		4)	4	4	18	9		4)	4	10	17	17
5)	3	6	12	9		5)	10	6	2	7		5)	4	0	12	18
Page 101	A	B	C	D		Page 102	A	B	C	D		Page 103	A	B	C	D
1)	7	12	12	13		1)	9	15	13	0		1	8	15	10	3
2)	17	5	9	9		2)	17	13	2	7		2	14	13	9	6
3)	11	8	8	12		3)	16	6	15	1		3	11	9	17	3
4)	4	6	11	9		4)	5	6	13	3		4	4	4	11	4
5)	10	12	14	9		5)	5	8	10	5		5	8	0	12	10

Answers (word problems page no 104 -106)

1)4   2)3   3)9   4)8   5)8   6)7   7)16   8)15   9)14   10)2   11)0   12)2   13)2   14)3   15)4
16)6   17)3   18)5   19)9   20)6   21)8   22)7   23)15   24)2   25)4

xxxxxxxxxxxxxxxxxxxxxxxxxxxxxxxxxxxxxxxxxxxxxxxxxxxxxxxxxxxxxxxxxxxxxxxxxxxxxxxxxxxx

Thank you for choosing Agnes Christy Maths books

Year 1 books

This book is volume 1 of the series for year 1 practice maths workbook. Look out for volume 2 practice maths book in Amazon, once you finish with this book.

Year 2 Books

Our bestselling books for year 2 reasoning are as follows. Available in Amazon

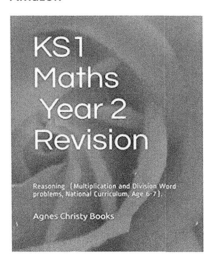

Agnes Christy Books (ACB)

Be kind to one another (Holy Bible)

Reward page

After completing each page ask your child to colour each box below or add a sticker.

1	2	3	4	5	6	7	8	9	10
You are a clever child	11	12	13	14	15	16	17	18	19
20	You are bright	21	22	23	24	25	26	27	28
29	30	31	32	33	34	35	You are intelligent	36	37
38	39	40	41	42	43	44	45	46	47
48	49	50	51	52	You are smart	53	54	55	56
57	58	59	60	61	62	63	64	65	66
67	68	You are a shining star	69	70	71	72	73	74	75
76	77	78	79	80	81	82	83	You are super	84
85	86	87	88	89	90	91	92	93	94
95	96	97	98	99	100	You are a genius	Well done	Wow great	You are a superstar

Printed in Great Britain
by Amazon

42859570R00064